Jesus is Back!

The Sun of God has risen in the West, in the city of Lost Angels.

By
Hazrat Isa Bin Maryam
Aka Muneer

Drawings by Christopher Broussard

Table of Contents

THE OPENING STATEMENT 3
INDUCTION 4
THE CREATION OF THE WHITE MAN 7
THE ABOMINABLE SNOWMAN 10
T.V. (FACT) OR (FICTION) 12
T.V. PITCHES 13
MORE NEWS 13
FROM GENETICS TO GROUND 15
WOMB OF MAN OR WOMBMAN 17
THE "NIGHTRIDERS" 19
THE OPPRESSOR 23
GO FIGURE 25
BLACK'S HAIR 27
MY MOTHER 28
AN ADDICT'S PRAYER 29
POETIC WISDOM 30
MY RECOVERY DISCOVERY 31
OUT THE WAY 33
THE FOOL 33
ATTENTION 34
THE FOG 36
WHO AM I? 37
THE MESSAGE 39
SAGACIOUSNESS 41
STRENGTH 42
I PONDER 42
ANCIENT PRACTICE 43
THE COLOR OF SPIRIT 44
THE 4TH DIMENSION 45
THE PROFESSIONAL VICTIM 46

THE SMART ASS	47
THE END RESULT	49
DICTIONARY	52
INNER FILTH	53
THE "JEALOUS" GOD	55
WE	59
ODE TO SCOTTY	61
POETIC WISDOM	65
THE FIGHT	65
HEAD TROUBLE	66
THE MOTH	67
THE ICY FIRE	69
THE FLY	71
THE FAIR WEATHER FRIEND	73
THE EPIPHANY OF THE PROPHET	74
AND AGAIN I WRITE	79
THE ADULT CHILD	80
TODAY'S LEARNING	81
THE QUEST	82
THE LOST AND TURNED OUT	82
LISTEN	83
THE WEED	84
FITTING IN	89
AT LONG LAST	89
AM I CRAZY?	90
NO MATTER	94
FLEETING LIFE	95
AUTHORS COMMENTS	97
666 THE MARK OF THE BEAST-UNLEASHED!	100

The Opening Statement

Of all containers in the world that you'd find,
None is harder to open than a closed mind.

Of all the shades of darkness that hinders man's sight,
None blinds more than the darkness of ignorance night.

Among man there exists the deepest of all pain,
It's the one felt by the descendent of Cain.

No one plays a bigger fool,
Than the man who sacrifices his integrity to be cool.

Induction

My eyes are dry I cry no more,
Yes I've been down this road before.

Like an alleged Shakespearean tale,
With sword me you'd impale.

Coerced by a violent drama,
Yarn dawned from a llama.

Eli Whitney's cotton gin at work,
A smile turned to a smirk.

Smug as thy expression may be,
Fanaticism dwells within thee.

Amidst all the dimensions and galaxies,
Exist one free of fallacies.

Turmoil scoffed forever and ever more,
Excavating for the peace of before.

Stylish, sassy clothing by Vidal Sassoon,
Brook's splendor lost in Blue Lagoon.

To thy equivocation do I relate,
For victory I shan't hesitate.

Eyes are fixed upon the prize,
Ego deflated to right size.

Perplexed by situations of a fool,
Over the universe can man rule.

Asleep within his psyche,
Lies the strength to be free.

Arise oh limitless leviathan called man,
Cooperate with the divine plan.

Heed the call to endless glory,
Bring to climax thy story.

Forbidden pleasure, innate bizarre desire,
Beckons man to hell's blazing fire.

Illuminate your soul with energy replete,
In righteousness against others compete!

Elevate thyself each living hour,
Expand your horizons with power.

Persist in seeking to do right,
Heed the Prophet of Light.

From thy lethargy it's time to awaken,
On the straight and narrow be taken.

Circumambulate Earth's Most Sacred House,
Be an example to thy spouse.

Lying deep inside the Holy Sanctuaries room,
Is a portal to the Originator, Savior from doom.

Should forgiveness be what you seek,
Then give it like the strong, the meek.

Wanting to escape consequence or repercussion,
Having fallen prey to subliminal seduction.

Revere the gifts given to thee,
Partake and receive what's free.

Be admonished oh ye scholar,
Hear the criers holler.

Beneath the treasure i.e. Cortez's gold,
A mystery awaits to be told.

Alike a Nubian or Amazonian queen,
So goes life's meticulous scene.

Romeo, Romeo where art thou today,
Wandering between shadows so they say.

Nimrod and Horus exploited our weak,
By their practice idols many seek.

Accursed by they claiming divinity,
In Babylon began the "Trinity".

This knowledge to some surprising,
Their beliefs based on hypothesizing.

Trapped in the vortex of a black hole,
Tunneling through constellations like a space mole.

Thought traveling at 24 billion miles per second,
Across galaxies I move when beckoned.

Arriving at truth's unrivaled destination,
Through the gift of desperation.

Perhaps alas man will attain sight,
Emerging into Sunrays from night.

Oh ye slaves of the sun,
The battle has begun.

No more will thy secrets protect you,
For you're in the category of the "*New*".

Among man is there hue,
Through they're merely a few.

Running rampant on third planet today,
Is evils epitome so they say.

Liberty beyond a living dream,
Bridging the gap with a seam.

Get attuned to pitch and frequency,
Overcoming thy spiritual delinquency.

Forget what you've been taught,
Through these pages truth is wrought.

**In the open of day or cover of night,
Heed these words with thy sight.**

The Creation of The White Man

Being madly angry that he was born,
From loving God he's found himself torn.

Having come about through sinful abomination,
A genetic mutant is his creation.

Physically different from hue-men,
Feeling deep pain are the *New*-men.

Having been welcome in every land,
Only to turn and bite their hand.

So we'll tell you the origin of the seed,
from which these new-men came to succeed.

One thing that the Torah (Old Testament) clearly shows us,
Is the evilness among the people of Moses.

After a time God refused to stand,
For those who practiced the wicked hand.

So on the evil was inflicted a disease,
which spread above and below the knees.

Leprosy was the name of the disease,
destroying their pigment as it damn well pleased.

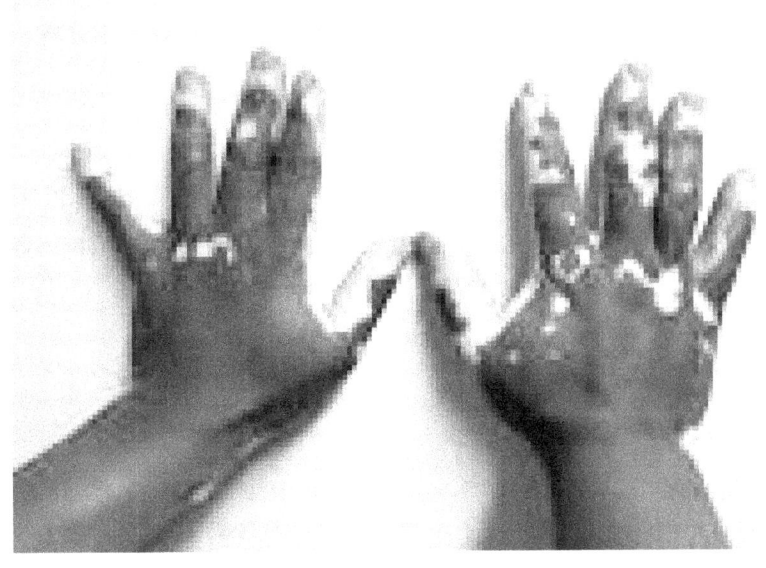

When each person became totally consumed,
Moses knew sealed was their fate – the doomed!

Having become a new type of man,
He had to be sent to another land.

So to the Caucus Mountains was he sent,
Where a period of gestation he underwent.

Evolving into a man totally new,
Having blond hair and eyes blue.

After getting stable on his feet,
From Europe he went the world to meet.

Lovingly did he the people greet,
knowing not that he was full of deceit.

Inherently knowing he's from an evil seed,
The *New*-Men are resentful indeed.

Living many are full of pain,
for the sun their skin can't tame.

**Among them Mercy is extended anew,
For those who's Spirit have gained some Hue.**

Many have been called yet only few are chosen,
For in vengeance, pain, and anger many are frozen.

We've just a story related to you
that sadly is very true.

Because of an endless hole through his middle,
The glory of God he does belittle.

Being madly angry that he was born,
From loving God he's found himself torn.

So we caution every one of you men,
That you prayerfully beware of the *New*–Men.

And now we must bring you up to speed,
for in all lands are the sinful seed.

What thou must come to terminate,
Is the production and harboring the thing called hate.

Should this in you be very great,
It may already be too late.

So others with increasing faithful skill,
Pray that God's way be you heal.

Love for you we truly feel,
That's why we keep it real.

Look, just because you may have some hue,
Doesn't mean you're free of the disease of the New.

So best is it you watch your step,
For in you the sickness may have crept.

The Abominable Snowman

There's a creature that's not just indigenous to
The Himalayan Mountains,
For in America he had "Whites Only" drinking fountains.

He's been known to throw a monkey wrench in a many plan,
And he's commonly called the Abominable Snowman.

To many folks he's told a lie,
By calling himself a white guy.

Portraying himself in films to be superior,
Truth is he's extremely inferior.

To prove this true we state fact one,
That his skin can't take the sun.

Yet he still devised a plan,
By inventing the fantasy of Superman.

Claiming to gain strength from a yellow sun,
Of tails and lies it's second to none.

Thru his soul a sickness does ravage,
This is why he's such a savage.

Of his character hate is the main feature,
Which distinguishes him apart from every creature.

So skillful he is at telling a lie,
That upon hearing it you'll begin to cry.

And when it comes to being slick,
He's a master of that trick.

A truth of him that history does render,
Is that he's known as the "Great Pretender".

His immoral values are plastered all over the tube,
Constantly embedded in the mind of the boob.

What we've stated may seem harsh or crude,
However the Snowman is a hellish dude.

Beware of his evil as best you can,
For he is the Abominable Snowman.

T.V. (Fact) or (Fiction)

Sex, violence, fear and greed,
Are any of these you in need?

If your goal is to be a neurotic boob,
Just sit and randomly watch the tube.

If you're tired of being free,
Be of those who watch T.V.

If control of your life you long to lose,
Then forget discretion when channels you choose.

To lose sight of whether you're coming or going,
Let T.V. teach you all of its knowing.

To buy into sorcery or magic,
the products of T.V. are tragic.

If you're committed to believing the lie,
Continue to get television a try.

Should you desire to be a mindless slave,
For T.V.'s worst programming just be brave.

If with reality you like a contradiction,
Then partake of regular or science fiction.

If you want your children to think they're grown,
Let them sit in front of T.V. and be shown.

T.V. Pitches

Product pitches on T.V.,
Targeting you and me.

Quick to give us a tale,
Hoping to make a sale.

Offering some type of relief,
In reality they're a thief.

Don't be a mindless boob,
Beware of the tube.

Product pitches on T.V.,
Targeting you and me.

More News

If you'd like a case of the blues,
Just sit and watch the news.

If you don't enjoy being free,
It may be because you watch T.V.

If fear, facts, and fiction you have yet to confuse,
Just keep watching the news.

If in the business of others you tend to be,
It may be because you watch T.V.

If you'd like to get the priorities of life twisted,
Just tune in to the programming as listed.

If touch with your child you'd like to lose,
Of television programming let him choose.

If your mind you'd like to abuse,
Just sit and watch the news.

Although conceived to be a helpful tool,
The uses of T.V. are by no means cool.

If you want to develop ignorance beyond mention,
Continue to give T.V. your attention.

If to fear and violence you'd like to be devout,
Then the regular watching of T.V. you need be about.

If to forgiving self and others you refuse,
It may be because you watch the news.

If to God's guidance you've found yourself astray,
Reconsider what we've told you today.

If you'd like a case of the blues,
Just sit and watch the news

From Genetics to Ground

The first book of the Bible is Genesis a.k.a. Genetics,
For the spirit uses the body as an advanced form of prosthetics.

In man lies a unique duality,
The highest and lowest forms of reality.

Foolishly claiming to be a literal child of God as impractical as that may be,
Having been born makes him a creature-created is he!

Never overcoming physical death,
An animated life form he is till his last breath.

Feeling highs, mediums and lows,
The limit of his potential only God knows.

Indeed many say that man is a creature of habit,
As seriously troubled as the hunter's rabbit.

As soon as he encounters some form of tragedy,
Man then forms his own strategy.

Hell is very patient and for man it does wait,
Those who reject God or Good manufacture ought but hate.

Parents, complexion or eye color not one of you did choose,
Nor does it have any bearing on whether you win or lose.

If Heaven you find yourself in,
Then surely you are of those who win.

Christ said: "The kingdom of heaven is within",
Therefore on earth does it begin.

The power to do good and refrain from evil comes only
From the One who sits on the throne,
By many names is the Creator called or known.

In order to make certain tools and appliances safe and sound,
The electric cord contains a third wire for ground.

From which a lesson of wisdom can be obtained,
For through electrical impulses work the body and brain.

When you're depressed or full of doubt,
Your head then needs to be grounded out.

Abraham, Moses, Jesus, Muhammad and others Peace did they attain,
For they prayed and worshiped faced down while grounding the brain.

Genesis 17:3 Abram bowed down with his face to the ground, and God said to him….

Numbers 16:22 But Moses and Aaron fell face down on the ground. "O God," they pleaded, "you are the God who gives…

Matthew 26:39 Jesus walked on a little way. Then he knelt with his face to the ground and prayed…..
(Prostrated)

THIS GUY IS NOT JESUS; HE IS *NOT* PRAYING ON HIS FACE!

For this means that Jesus prayed regularly on his face. To do so only once when in desperation would make him a hypocrite. A Christian is supposed to be someone who imitates Christ; Right? In what religion do people pray on their Face?

Womb of man or Wombman

In the beginning man the Devil did deceive,
Through his weakness known as Eve.

Every man save Adam you can safely presume,
Was born from the darkness called Womb.

Surely ye have been had,
If you believe sexual reproduction is bad.

Every culture from early times till this day,
Pursues the sex relation in its own way.

Yet who would have thought or could even believe,
That Satan would attack through the descendants of Eve.

The soundness or strength of every nation,
Rests on the respect of the Womb-man not her degradation.

The wise and the wicked have long believed,
In the enormous influential power stored within Eve.

Though man was created from mud specially molded into shape,
His fleshly drives alone he can't escape.

One thing that's been overlooked but has long been known,
Is that Woman was created from bone.

The backbone or strength of every nation, family, or society,
Is known as the Spirited female body.

From one person to another,
She is generally known as mother.

With her lies and immensely important duty,
That the task of rearing and raising little Bob or Judy.

Very strong is she we tell you no lie,
For Wombman can bleed a week and not die!

The "Nightriders"
(27 Ramadan 2013)
(Los Angeles, California)

Now it's time to firmly discuss,
How the "Homeless" ride the bus.

Although this is in the early time,
Written these words are in rhyme.

The sky is our ceiling the ground our floor,
Having no walls we're free to explore.

No shelters have we to rest,
Faced are we with a test.

We ride buses all the night long,
To no apartment or house do we belong.

Our bodies we feed and clean while day,
We nightriders have nowhere to stay.

Sons, daughters, grandmothers and fathers,
Earth is our address the weather our bothers.

In houses you work, rest, and play,
Whilst we have no place to stay.

For man to acquire balance,
He need help us with our challenge.

MTA lines 33, 60, and 20 are a few,
Of which we ride the night through.

Some operators having compassion let us stay,
On the bus throughout their layover each day.

In the midnight hour we cry for more,
The beach of homelessness is our shore.

Some operators are heartless do we say,
For they air-condition the bus the whole way.

Knowing no house have we found,
Freezing us is evilly unsound.

Putting us off at layover buses end,
To us homeless they're truly no friend.

Some of us are very tired and old,
So by God their stories now told.

Rather than sleep on the cement ground,
On buses we nightriders are found.

Yet when we need stretch out our legs and head,
On cardboard and concrete we rest our head.

Many of us are mentally ill and unable,
To maintain or secure housing that's stable.

Our spirit cries out with a yelp,
O family please give us your help!

In order for man to thwart Satan's plan,
Through action he need love his fellow man.

To overcome the evil's plot,
Man must share what he's got.

With words he states a loving poise,
Yet he is only making mere noise.

If to his brethren love he doesn't show,
In hell fire him will God throw.

So many sleep soundly (at home) during the night,
Whilst we the nightriders suffer our plight.

Ramadan is the month of burning,
So for our well-being you'd be yearning.

Through this writing you we call and warn,
Desist your self-righteous homeless scorn.

Should for paradise you yearn,
Compassion, selflessness you need learn.

Of complaints do you have an abundant supply,
Sleeping under roofs whilst we have only the sky.

So when to ingratitude you are faithful,
Recall the plight of the nightriders to be grateful.

Yes o people who have food, clothing, and shelter,
Beware of the ultimate Helter Skelter.

Trickin Self

**Haloween 2018 Trick? Or Treat?
Is when this book was published**

When you specialize in being slick,
On yourself you play a trick.

If from God you seek His power,
Daily you should pray for an hour.

Should you pray ten minutes six times a day,
Rest assured you're on your way.

If you make a mockery of God's guidance,
You're destined for hell and its violence.

When on your knees you neglect to fall,
Then on Satan do you really call.

If you want freedom from this place,
Then you need pray on your face.

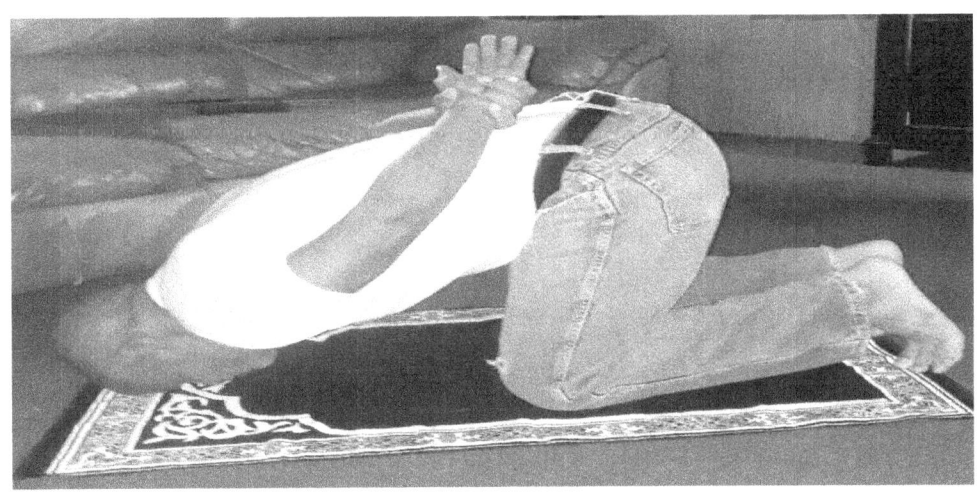

Should this to you sound very strange,
Then you seriously need to change.

So if you desire to be truly free,
Just heed the words that come from me.

Remember when you specialize in being slick,
On yourself you but play a trick.

The Oppressor
(The world bankers who stole and corrupted the term Illuminati)

From sea to shining sea, from Canada to Mexico there it is –
America!

Who sets the standards for the free?
Who determines how you will be you and me-me?

The Illuminati – the few but powerful elite,
Out of our freedom us did they cheat.

We are the most willing slaves in history,
For we think it's natural you see.

For freedom we don't even long,
For we believe as slaves we belong.

Pursuing what's socially acceptable,
The Blacks and Hispanics trying to be White,

Yet warring on one another like it's right.
So many have eyes yet not a lick of sight.

Being ever so busy chasing our tail,
From our true purpose we've come to fail.

Wallowing in emotionalism and a material compulsion,
Of truth and purposeful living we haven't a notion.

Consuming the evil potion just because,
We think we are in need of a buzz.

Following the dimmest of light,
Being held by one who isn't right.

Unaware of the doom,
Until in life there's no more room.

Out of time to live, not aware of our foolish flare;
Now for God and truth we care,
Yet into oblivion do we stare.

So many are caught in the oppressor's snare,
And for heaven they don't want a share.

But it's too late now,
For death wields a relentless plow.

It's now time for the end of your life,
Say goodbye to the husband, the wife.
That's it, that's your life!

In the Los Angeles county Jail there was immense corruption,
Inmates were allowed cash, this created the disruption.

The solution was very simple,
Money was removed like a popped pimple.

In many lands people practice a way,
That eliminates evil to this day.

With the system of bartering one can't lose,
Trading or exchanging as two or more choose.

Fair exchange is no robbery as the parties agreed,
Without money people comfortably succeed!

Go Figure

A unique paradox to figure,
Is why Blacks called each other "Nigger".

For if called one by a Hispanic, Asian, or White,
Blacks are ready to fight.

Of the names putting down any other race,
No name can catch or take "Nigger's" place.

And another things that's a switch,
Is how their women call each other "Bitch".

To one another they exclaim,
These names to themselves without shame.

Of "Bitch" and "Nigger" they're so proud,
They use these terms out loud.

No matter if it's love or anger they want to show,
The words "Bitch" and "Nigger" they throw.

Indeed it seems hard to understand,
What has happened to the so-called Black Man.

There's just no way to sensibly state,
Why Blacks to each other this way relate.

However we have come to find,
That many are senselessly flying blind.

Indeed it's a unique paradox to figure,
Why Blacks call each other "Bitch" and "Nigger".

Black's Hair

Unhappy with their share,
So they seek European hair.

Unable to comprehend the kink,
So how to straighten their hair they think.

In spite of what they profess to know,
They behave like an Oreo.

Against a sisters hair they fight,
Pretending that they are white.

It's a sad sight to see,
What's happened to the sister of you and me.

From hot combs and perms to wigs and weave,
Their birth hair's texture they leave.

So much time, energy and care,
Is put into the production of hair.

It just doesn't seem right,
Why they struggle to be white.

What seems to be very great,
Is a feeling for self called hate.

**Alas arise oh Nubian Queen,
To thy self be true not mean.**

**Lift up your Natural with pride,
For in you does God reside**

My Mother

One person's special to me unlike any other,
That's the one who's known as My Mother.

She'll always be my favorite Girl,
A uniquely Priceless and Precious Pearl.

Connected we are on a level so deep,
That into my heart she can peep.

And when from each other we are miles away,
I feel her with me every day.

About me much has she worried,
For down hells road I've hurried.

Unlike any other relative or any friend,
My love for Mommy will never end!

She'll always be near and dear to me,
In spite of where she or I maybe.

One person's special to me unlike any other,
That's the one who's known as My Mother.

Many have turned against me with hate,
But Mama would always lovingly wait.

Care for me she hasn't failed to do,
In spite of the pain I put her through.

And when I was hooked on dope,
Even then she never lost hope.

Then when my scorecards read zero,
Into action went My Mother my hero.

During the times I was lost in a maze,
Mama said: "don't worry son there'll be better days".

Next to God -She's who I give praise,
For loved me she has through every phase.

To me there's one person above every other,
The Most Beautiful Girl in the world– **My Mother!**

An Addict's Prayer

Lord help me won't you please,
Rid me of this horrid disease.

Please show me where to start,
And rid the evil from my heart.

Free me from my earthly desire,
Liberate me from Hell's fire.

Grant me Thy Grace and Power,
Change me this very hour.

Stop me from having a busy mind,
Grant me release from fear's bind.

Illuminate the path I am to travel,
Help me sidestep the judge's gavel.

Lord tell me what I am to do,
Please let me hear from You.

In You Lord my faith does belong,
Help me Lord make me strong.

At times I doubt and feel weak,
Please make me humble and meek.

Improve in me my writing skill,
Help me do Your Powerful Will.

Parting can be such sweet sorrow,
Who knows what lies in tomorrow.

Thank You Lord for removing the dope,
Thank You Lord for giving me hope.

Poetic Wisdom

With every struggle there always comes ease,
Even when you battle a deadly disease.

Every soul has a burden of which to bear,
For the sake of others do you care?

If thoughts of self you have currently consumed,
Then you are currently one of the doomed.

When you help others for a return favor,
Then the devil's your lord and savior.

Should your good deeds be based on self,
Then you're no more than Satan's elf.

If being good is too much trouble,
You need ask God's help on the double.

When on righteousness one can't stand,
Then Satan has you in his hand.

In order to see self and not some story,
Then you need take a moral inventory.

My Recovery Discovery

Over time I made a discovery,
No religion comes before my recovery.

After many hard knocks this truth was found,
Following religious attempts I'd tweak on the ground.

At the Bible and the Qur'an addiction did laugh,
I didn't know that spiritually I needed a bath.

Then after praying in the Mosque 8 rakats (parts) to the east,
Still I smoked kitty litter, white specks and even yeast.

In Church I was dipped, dunked, and practically drowned,
And still in my mouth a pipe was found.

And after reading John, Luke, Timothy or even Mark,
To a crack pipe I still put a spark.

After being "Born Again and Saved" many times though sincere and brave,
To drug use I was still a slave.

Many an opportunity my addiction did kill,
Dozens were hurt by my self-will.

In order for the future my recovery to extend,
For harms done to all I must amend.

Another thing I must continue to do,
Is inventory myself excluding you!

Helping others is the highlight of my day,
Through words and actions there's much I say,

Another thing of which I made a discovery,
The word "Bill" is Arabic for RECOVERY.

**My life has been renewed I let you know,
And through 12-step living I continue to grow.**

Over time I made a very big discovery, Now no religion comes before my recovery!

Out the Way

The best I can do each day,
Is to simply stay out the way.

Prayerfully seeking God's Will all day long,
Meditation and prayer keeps me focused and strong.

Acting as a witness of God by praise,
My behavior preaches His Word all my days.

My life is no longer a confusing maze,
Nor is my mind consumed by a haze.

Out to the Lord do I reach,
And through me, you He does teach.

No longer is life a great big joke,
Nor does my life go up in smoke.

Prayerfully seeking God's will all day long,
Meditation and prayer keeps me focused and strong.

The best I can do each day,
Is to simply stay out the way.

The Fool

You're so busy trying to be hip, slick, and cool,
That you're no more than a fool.

Of worldly ways are you curious,
Of serving God you're not serious.

Life is not a joke or a game,
So quit being a seeker of Fame.

Instead of spending so much time at play,
Increase your efforts ten-fold to pray.

The joys of this world will not last,
You need to be of those who truly fast.

As to why you use this or that nickname,
You're merely glorifying self, seeking fame.

Trying to be hip, slick, and cool,
Stop playing the part of the fool.

Contrary to popular belief,
Through surrender you get relief.

Be an Indian and let God be the chief,
Then and only then will you get relief.

Attention

The time is now for us to mention,
The extent some will go just for attention.

Seeking to be in the popularity class,
Willing to make of themselves an ass.

Being silly they will show,
To any lengths they'll go.

Spiritual steps act as a prevention,
Against the silly pursuit of attention.

Some people refuse to grow,
Thriving on the focus of self that others show.

Quick to make a foolish spectacle of them self,
For praise and focus they'll be Satan's elf.

Delving into the unknown,
Behaving like right they haven't been shown.

Then in the name of a good laugh,
in raw sewage they'll take a bath.

For a spot on TV,
There is nothing they won't be.

Whether it's being a class clown,
Or showing others that you're "down".

Seeking glory and fame,
In hopes of establishing for self a name.

To be a fool's dead ringer,
They'll gladly go on Jerry Springer.

Causing humiliation, suffering and pain,
Trampling over the feelings of others for a moment's "fame".

What benefit to you is the acquisition of attention?
No more than what we just mentioned.

We hope again we won't have to mention,
The extent some will go just for attention.

The Fog

Between man and God exist a clog,
Seen and referred to as "The Fog".

Those who are "God wise",
Can see the fog in others eyes.

For it is a cloudy cataract like formation,
From which is no light emanation.

It is also commonly known,
That the befogged are in a "Dead Zone".

Indeed their world has been rocked,
For they are spiritually blocked.

Drifting in the realm of the unknown,
Frightened; feeling all alone.

In a darkness no one wants to call home,
Unable to perceive light they but roam.

Like all the lost they think along a flat plane
So their minds have come to freeze,
While the righteous excel for they think in degrees.

Those who reside in the realm of the fog,
Experience the torment of the bog.

Between man and God exist a clog,
Seen and referred to as "The Fog".

Who Am I?

Once under my spell
You'll enter Hell,
Who am I?

Once under my spell to yourself you'd lie,
Who am I?

Once under my spell
No one a thing to you can tell,
Who am I?

Once under my spell
You'll succeed to fail,
Who am I?

Once under my spell
You'll experience the burning of Hell,
Who am I?

Once under my spell you'll fall to your knees
And do as I please,
Who am I?

Once under my spell the good of your life will die,
Who am I?

Once under my spell pain you'll feel
For I am very real,
Who am I?
Once under my spell having no peace
You'll vainly seek release,
Who am I?

Once under my spell you're truly lost
Cause I'm the boss,
Who am I?

Once under my spell for relief you'll yearn
Cause painful is my burn,
Who am I?

Once under my spell I'll pull your string
Like a puppet thing,
Who am I?

Once under my spell I'll destroy your life
Inflicting on you strife,
Who am I?

Once under my spell you're a resident of hell,
Who am I?

Once under my spell the truth you'll take to be a lie,
Who am I?
Now that you're hopelessly under my spell,
The truth to you now I tell:

You need a 12 step program to break my spell.
Who am I?

**I am
Your Diseased Mind!**

The Message

The Message of A.A.'s: "Reverend" James
Bland
(R.I.P.)

If "LIFE'S" lesson; You've been missen,
It's because You need LEARN TO LISTEN.

For the enjoyment of "LIFE" You to have a turn,
You need LISTEN TO LEARN.

In order for You to really grow,
You must stop thinking You "no".

When for Your actions on all but SELF You place blames,
You need heed the "Message" of: "Reverend" James.

When about Your circumstance You complain,
Then You need LEARN to be: "SANE".

Should with ALCOHOL, i.e. D.R.U.G.S. You wet Your whistle,
You may need Read: **Dr. Silkworth's Epistle.**

If due to drinking/using Your "LIFE" continues to ' fall '
You may be in need of a "12 STEP CALL".

In order for Your "LIFE" to begin anew,
LEARN TO LISTEN You **must** do**!**

To experience "THE PEACE" we all YEARN,
You definitely must LISTEN TO LEARN.

Thus: You have to **LEARN TO LISTEN** so You can LISTEN TO LEARN,
Whereby the entrance of "HEAVEN" You'll have a turn.

D.R.U.G.S. means:
"Devils Revenge Upon God's Servants"

Good D.R.U.G.S. means:
Doing Recovery Under God's Supervision

Sagaciousness

A feat greater than any of Houdini,
The cleansing of the mysterious Kundalini.

It's the dawn of a new age,
Heed the words of this sage.

The twilight of darks day is upon us,
Never the less humans still fuss.

Each new day starts as night,
Yet man argues about being right.

From simple news to stressful blues,
Which path will one choose.

The juggernaut of self-will is subsiding,
Thru the chakras pure powers gliding.

Meditation on breath taken to great length,
With fasting and prayer comes pure strength.

Mans largest opponent is simply he,
Today my best friend is me!

Strength

On and off throughout each day,
Remember your Lord and continue to pray.

Listen not to Satan's sinister calls,
And your soul will take no falls.

Be grateful to God every day,
And praise and thanks be sure to say.

Should Satan cause you sorrow and fear,
Remember your Lords always near.

Although the evil have a plan,
God's stronger than any man.

So when you dismayed or troubled at length,
Call on your Lord He'll give you strength.

I Ponder

As I sit and look around the room,
I stop and ponder each man's doom.

What is it that stands in his way,
That keeps him off his knees today?

Will he ever be one who succeeds,
Found heavy in his righteous deeds?

As I sit and look around the room,
I stop and ponder each man's doom.

Ancient Practice

For information that's in-depth and vast,
You get when you meditate and fast.

The universe's secrets are revealed,
Mysteries no more concealed.

Attaining Peace which surpasses all understanding,
Your body healing per your commanding.

If ascetic practice be your goal,
You're to achieve self-control.

Heightening the six sense power,
Over lower desires you tower.

Ability to take troubles in stride,
Freedom found on the inside.

For information that's in-depth and vast,
Just simply meditate and fast.

The Color of Spirit

Back and forth do they debate,
They claim that God caused hate.

This is what we won't take,
For their tales are truly fake.

**For those who can hear it,
The truth is God is Spirit.**

Spirit can't be touched or seen,
Do you know what we mean?

First off if **God** became a man,
Commandment **1** couldn't stand!

Secondly to prove this true,
Does **Spirit** eat like you?

If this step did **He** take,
Made would **He** have a mistake.

If a color did **He** choose,
Many a man would **He** confuse.

Jesus had a color and race, No man has seen **God's Face**!

The 4th Dimension

Whether you'd be Christian, Muslim or Jew,
Fundamentally the same are each of you.

The fourth dimension of existence is open to all just the same,
even to the atheist, agnostic or those under a religious name.

The power which animates the body is called Spirit,
No one can see, touch or hear it.

For its presence is very real,
commonly sensed by those who can feel.

Spirit is the cause of all vibration,
Ultimately known as the core of creation

There are two words which chain the mind,
That'll forever keep you blind.

The words "I know" are they,
hindering you from the "Way".

How quick many are to beg or ask God to forgive them,
yet they refuse to forgive those they condemn.

How dare you ask for that which you refuse to give,
In a world consisting of selfish, self-serving demands do you live.

Love is an action emanating from selfless motives deep within,
Pride less self-sacrificing for another over and again.

Happy are they, who reside in the realm of the Spirit,
For they are doers of the word, not just ones who hear it.

Today in life many merely seek an emotional peak,
Due to the nature of feelings, emotional instability is all they wreak.

Feelings, emotions aren't facts we tell you no lie,
For they come and go like clouds in the sky.

The Professional Victim

The systems always out to lick them,
Are the cries of the professional victim.

An abundance of excuses are in his vault,
Exclaiming "It's always someone else's fault".

Through his vision he is shown,
"They won't leave him alone".

Fast is he to repeatedly shout,
"They keep singling me out!"

If the world would just leave him be,
"I'll be alright", so says he.

Creating excuses and alibis are his forte,
From New York City to Duarte.

From border to border and coast to coast,
"I'm innocent" Is his boast.

The systems always out to lick them,
Are the cries of the professional victim.

The Smart Ass

No one likes a smart ass,
For when it comes to words he has the last.

Steadily focus on being right,
Causing an argument and or fight.

Steeped in pride in the air of arrogance he'll stay,
For truly to God's Path he can't find his way.

His haughtiness blinds him to see,
That God he will never be.

Playing God is so hard to do,
For the world and its people just won't obey you.

If indeed peace you like to pursue,
Then God playing you must be through.

In order to have the cataracts removed which hamper thy sight,
Cease trying to be right, and ponder what's right.

After the surgery before you can see,
You'll begin to experience peace and harmony.

Erie is the way of which things work,
A beautiful swan from an ugly duckling jerk.

Public humiliation of the outside man,
Is often God sculpting a beautiful inner man.

Now we mention something that's a gas,
That beauty of form in time will pass.

Then again we'll say because it's true,
That inner beauty endures eternally through.

It's written that God's Sight is thousands of times brighter than the sun,
Therefore His Vision can't be comprehended by anyone.

In the unveiled presence of God no man can stand,
Nor can anyone be or grow without His Hand.

Ungracefully angered because He's God and you're not,
Is the root of the devil man's sinister plot.

Savage is the man who won't pray,
Except when he wants his way.

No one likes a smart ass,
For when it comes to words he has the last.

Steadily focused on being right,
Causing an argument and or fight.

The End Result

When about your life do you complain,
Hardship and suffering you'll always sustain.

Such a deep sadness afflicting you,
A morbid attraction in hell's zoo.

Unaware that you're merely a man,
Thinking your God you continuously plan.

Yet when things don't go as expected,
To pain and sorrow you're deeply connected.

As a charlatan in life making your own way,
A versed hypocrite ever you'll stay.

Engulfed by a disease of the mind,
Carrying on like one of the blind.

A citizen of the world of stagnation,
Temporary pleasure is thy contemplation.

In search of a momentary thrill,
Your brother's character your words kill.

Gossiping and backbiting hearing not what you say,
The flesh of thy brother you eat with the words you say.

A man can preach till he turn the deepest of the color blue,
Never able to heal the sickness buried within you.

Locked on a destination deep within hell,
Things to you no one can tell.

Believing that knowledgeable you are so much,
Refusing the love of those with the healing touch.

So seriously are you self-deceived,
In God you really never have believed.

Stimulated by the overt lie,
For the pleasures of this world you cry.

Thinking that for your sins you have a waiver,
Because you're told for you died Christ the Savior.

This brings us to point out to you,
That which already you know to be true.

If indeed the price for sin were paid,
Then your heart guilt wouldn't raid.

When about your life you do complain,
Hardship and suffering you'll always sustain.

Running life on your own will,
Subject are you to be road kill.

Sorry indeed are they,
Viewing life as something to play.

Treating the guidance of God as an infomercial,
Regarding this life like a dress rehearsal.

Until death the next level is virtually unknown,
Save for those in whose heart-s heaven is home.

So what can anyone say to the waywardly wicked ever astray?

Growing up emotionally you can't do,
Spiritually petrified the fire awaits you.

When about your life you do complain,
Hardship and suffering you'll always sustain.

Shall you be a slave to instinctual desire,
Subject are you to be a cheat, thief, and liar.

If to get money sex is used as a tool,
Subjected are you to twisted desirous rule.

When to acquire sex moneys used as a tool,
Devoid of compassion you're so cruel.

As though atop a dangerously high wire,
Hard it is to balance desire.

When about your life you do complain,
Hardship and suffering you'll always sustain.

Dictionary

Just in case you haven't heard,
There's a difference between reading and reading word for word.

To overcome ignorance without a doubt,
Read with a dictionary roundabout.

Stop thinking you can define a word based on how it's read,
And use a dictionary to get ahead.

Often your actions scream aloud,
Of your behavior which is proud.

Quick to think that something you know,
Trying thy best others this to show.

So fearful of being thought of or called a dupe,
That further into ignorance you stoop.

Like a dog chasing his tail,
Thoroughly you succeed to fail.

So concerned with what others may think,
That you flush your life right down the drink.

Continuing to put up a front for a show,
Trying to convince others that you "Know".

Having spent years perfecting the prestigious art,
Of convincing people that you're smart.

Carrying on in an effort to be cool,
You but play the Court Jester- the Fool!

In order for your growth to proceed,
You need to understand what you read.

Using a dictionary is definitely work,
Yet it beats the hell out of being a jerk.

Stop trying to look so damn good,
And start asking questions like you should.

So worried about looking bad that living are you in fear,
Misunderstanding most of what you read or hear.

Busy are you ever so much,
That with the truth you're out of touch.

Overly concerned with how you look,
Frivolous is the mission you took.

If with wisdom and higher learning you'd like to marry,
Then pickup Webster's dictionary!

In order to enhance your mind,
We recommend a dictionary of the collegiate kind.

To quickly boost your knowledge,
Collegiate merely means that of college.

Inner filth

Just because one says their Muslim, Christian, or Jew,
Does not mean he is one of you.

Even those who say they're in recovery,
May not be into Bill's discovery.

The seventh level the lowest in Hell,
Is for those called hypocrites the truth we tell.

For their actions speak against their words,
And into hell they'll be driven in herds.

Often do you witness a man's lips moving unable to hear a word he's saying,
For oppositely opposed is the message his actions relaying.

The hypocrites do not respect you,
for to themselves they aren't true,
Dangerous are these men who walk amongst you.

For they are but descendants of Cain,
And of those who feel naught but pain.

For on earth they wish to remain,
the pleasures of this life they wish to maintain.

Beware of those with smiling faces;
many are in a Spiritual stasis.

Steadily joking and or having fun,
are the practices of Adam's son.

Looking first to be accepted then to stand out in the crowd,
The descendants of Cain are obnoxious and loud.

Manifesting a weak, fake ass laugh,
refusing to give their Spirit a bath.

Although their outsides appear clean,
Playing God they're nice or mean.

If only life would go as expected,
to happiness they think they'll be connected.

Steadily smiling in your face,
secretly conspiring to take your place.

Smiling in your face,
Claiming human is their race.

Stating that their love is true,
Truth is they're just using you.

When it comes to loyal, unselfish concern for another,
to the idea of love they sigh saying "Oh brother".

One can't give what he does not have;
truly his Spirit needs a bath.

Competing in games to be the best,
Unaware of the Spirit within his breast.

If the message did you miss,
It's cause you need a catharsis.

The "Jealous" God

Among those calling themselves God's people are there some who believe the Greatest Lie,
That the Immortal, All Pure Creator became defiled and did die.

In order to understand the English translated versions of Bible although they vary,
You must consult the Oxford or Webster's dictionary.

However this Truth some won't believe,
For they wish to stay deceived.

Their argument against the real proof,
Keeps them from seeing or knowing the Truth.

Unable to even understand their own talk,
In endless circles do they walk.

Thinking along a flat plain their minds have come to freeze,
While the righteous excel for they think in degrees.

Oh what great havoc the devil has come to reek,
In the foolishly feeble minds of the weak.

Beware of those who say "The Bibles God's word,
The dictionary's man's word,
Ignorantly repeating what they've heard.

Both books are printed and published by man,
Words that have no meaning ye can't understand!

Trapped in the coils of the serpent a wicked teacher,
Unable to breath – suffocating as slaves of the wicked preacher.

With the devil many religious teachers do conspire,
Boldly racing each other to the fire.

Every word of each land do people seek to understand,
So their meanings are gathered in a book to help man.

What we offer is a powerful tool,
Whereby you can get free of corrupt rule.

In nearly every English translated version of the "Holy Bible",
Lies the key to escape Satan your enemy rival.

In the section called the Testament of Old,
An uncontested description of God is told.

One word holds the power to refute,
About that which many dispute.

The idea of God having begotten a son,
Is the basis for which wars are and have begun.

Brother hating and killing brother behind the Divinity,
Being argued and stated as "One in a Trinity".

Now we call to your attention once again,
To the Laws given to Moses of which there are Ten.

The first of which who,
Divides the False from the True.

"Hear O Israel, I the Lord thy God am a jealous God".
Is the opening statement in the First of the Ten,
In the Old Testament "Jealous God" is mentioned again and again.

What we're about to say will cause some to get hot,
For we will shine light on history's darkest plot.

So now we once again,
We call your attention to the First of Ten.

"We're not to make any graven images, or worship anything in the heaven above,
The earth beneath or the water under the earth".

Through the Laws given to Moses,
God very clearly told us,
The falsehood His Word exposes.

First we must point out,
The meaning of the word "Jealous" without a doubt.

It defined as: "intolerant of rivalry or associates".
Rivalry is competition and associates are partners as Webster's does define,
Sending what message to the mind?

**That God does not share His Throne,
For He is God alone!**

**Not putting up with partners makes He,
Free of being a Trinity.**

Secondly, God is perfect and would never contradict Himself,
Either openly or by stealth.

Hang on for we are about to explain to thee,
Facts to clear up the mystery.

That has shrouded a many a man,
Denying him Truth upon which to stand.

The three states of "matter" solid, liquid, and gas,
We were told not asked,
Through the first Law that to Moses was passed - Not to worship!

So we've begun to expose fold by fold,
The Greatest Lie ever told.

The human body alas,
Is made of solid, liquid, and gas.

Such a masterful work of fiction,
To say God is guilty of contradiction.

For if God were to become a man,
The first Law of Moses couldn't stand.

Steeped in darkness many shout,
That God is Jesus without a doubt.

So what question we have to ask of you,
To clarify the False from the True.

Does God pray to Himself ?

**Prayer is a petition, a request, or manner of asking;
God is the Creator and Owner of everything The Everlasting,
Of His self-*nothing* He'd be asking.**

We

The evil and the ignorant tell a lie,
for they misinterpret A form of I

Although they have done something sly,
we will pull the wool off your eye.

The time has come for all to see,
us and our are another form of we.

In order to get free of the idiocy,
to their teaching you have to say pui.

Sure we means Two, Three, or even more,
however many believe in mere folklore.

To get down into the core,
you'll need consider what you haven't before.

**They say that God is one in three,
so let's look at definition 2 of we.**

The second meaning of "**We**" is simply:

I

Used by writers, Sovereign, and God on high!

Ode to Scotty

From the "Godfather" of
C. A., A.A., and N.A.
Scotty
(R.I.P.)

Ages ago the Devil devised a plan,
On how to destroy the inner man.

The Prophecy of Moses shall we explain,
Known to many as A.b.e.l. killed by C.a.i.n.

But before we decode the acronymic encryptions,
We will bring to mind some its depictions.

Moses had foretold what we'll reveal as the basics,
Of what has come to be the real matrix.

Within the last century messages were sent and
programming was done openly and secretly,
Now is a fact history.

To the conscious and subconscious was said,
That which still remains in the head.

"Coca-Cola and Salt Rocks" were early on the scene,
Until in America in became an illegal thing.

Soon came other powerful whisperings,
That to the heart evil sings.

The introduction of "Rock n Roll" was a seductive thing,
Accompanied by "Rock star" idol worship did they bring.

So the most popular songs were called "Hits",
And many were told "Coke is it".

Rock worship soon became a popular thing,
And in the lyrics of various artists lied a poisonous sting.

"Cause I'm stone in love with you",
"Rock n roll is here to stay",
"I want a rock right now".

To name just a few,
Couple with sinister television programming too.
<u>Especially one about a certain family:</u>

The man who was the head,
Slept in a rock bed.

His wife was no louse,
And they lived in a rock house.

To get to work which wasn't far,
He drove a rock car.

And so they would not have to worry,
He worked in a rock quarry.

His watch was a sundial clock,
And he resided in the city of Bedrock.

**The only character capable of handling the stone,
Fred Flintstone is how he's known.**

Now we refer back to the word of Moses,
Wherein the future he shows us.

If the subject matter haven't you attained,
What we're talking about is cocaine.

Hidden in the revelation from Moses,
Is a stem of thorns accompanying today's roses.

For he revealed that C.A.I.N. killed A.B.E.L.,
A two fold truth not a fable.
As we have seen the destructive power,
Of the crack people devour.

For crack is highly purified cocaine chips,
Over which many a man trips.

For crack is highly purified cocaine chips,
Over which many a man trips.

C A I N has and does kill a man from being A B E L
R L N E   To bring food to the table.   B A P I
Y K D U   S L I F
S A U R   O A C E
T L C O   L N U
A L I S   U C R
L O N I   T E I
L I G S   Y D N
I D
E S

CAIN does kill men from being ABEL
To live a life that is stable.

Many sing that "Coke is the real T H I N G ".
                                                                      E I N A I
                                                                      R D S T F
                                                                      R D I U T
                                                                      O E D R S
                                                                      R N E E
                                                                           S

And soon discover with teeth grit,
The true meaning of "Coke is it".

And so we say thank you Moses,
For the truth your Prophecy exposes.

Poetic Wisdom

With every struggle there always comes ease,
Even when you battle a deadly disease.

Every soul has a burden of which to bear,
For the sake of others do you care?

If thoughts of self you have currently consumed,
Then you are currently one of the doomed.

When you help others for a return favor,
Then the devil's your lord and savior.

Should your good deeds be based on self,
Then you're no more than Satan's elf.

If being good is too much trouble,
You need ask God's help on the double.

When on righteousness one can't stand,
Then Satan has you in his hand.

In order to see self and not some story,
Then you need take a moral inventory.

The Fight

Acquisition of things referred to as wealth,
Seemingly more important than health.

Many have had their focus swayed,
Through empty hope and promise portrayed.

Influenced by stare at television,
Self-separations done in precision.

Families finely torn apart,
Per someone's sick art.

From which comes and incandescent red.
Impending maven in one's head.

A massacre of propitious spirituality,
Provoking cadets of brutality.

Arise old ye valiant knight,
Usher in the freeing fight.

Head Trouble

In life from birth till end,
One's enemy resides within.

Having a history of being on your shoulders
but not your friend,
Thy head gets you into trouble again and again.

Then insanely with the ease that you blink,
You quickly rely on what you think.

To some it's been a mystery,
Yet a constant fact of history.

That unbridled pride and instincts conspire,
To place you well within the fire.

The Gamble

If through your possessions you'd like to ramble,
Then continue to be of those who gamble.

And when with self you can't be trusted,
Perhaps it's because you play till you're busted.

Should you generate tons of disgust and hate,
It's because you play until it's too late.

So if you want your life in shambles,
Just continue to be one who gambles.

If the tendency to play is very great,
Words of wisdom will we relate.

In order to have peace from this sin,
When it comes to gambling surrender to win.

The Moth

Although Truth is distasteful to a man who's bitter,
The moth is attracted to lights glitter.

To God's Revelations many a man scoff,
For he rejects the way of the moth.

Dissuaded from light of any kind,
Attracted man is to darks blind.

Scampering about as though he is free,
Like the moth he refuses to be.

When in the midst of darkness appears the light,
Toward it always the moth takes flight.

Bearing witness to the oneness of God each of his days,
Throughout his life the moth sings God's praise.

In order for man to be right,
He must parallel the moth's flight.

As soon as he perceives a degree of light,
The moth is quick to escape the night.

Having what's called a compound eye,
Toward light he's quick to fly.

If to the wool over your eyes the moth hasn't met,
Be prayerfully patient awaiting it yet.

When he devours the wool setting thy eyes free,
Then truly God the Light you'll begin to see.

However if on Satan does a man call,
Blocked is he from being free by a mothball.

Then he will surely remain blind,
Unable to perceive light of any kind.

So if you long to be truly free,
Permit the most generous moth to help thee.

When the wooly pleasures of life have you blind,
Thru the moth God's merciful and kind.

The Icy Fire
(Written During Ramadan 2006)

On earth there isn't nothing at all nice,
about being burned by dry ice.

Now to you another truth we'll tell,
about level five of that called Hell.

For it is of an extreme cold,
for those who are arrogantly bold.

To those who to God turn a shoulder that's cold,
Beware of the torment of the abode.

For those who to their parents were not nice,
are destined to the place of hot ice.

Being of a Divine level of cold,
its temperature to you can't be told.

Unless ye repent, amend thy soul and hit thy knees,
you'll be of those in the fiery freeze!

Throughout the body will be a cracking and popping sound,
For deafening is the cold profound.

From the ends of the body and through the middle,
Will sound the shrieking of an untuned fiddle.

So to thy parents kindness need be kept,
and to being arrogantly bold you need sidestep.

Again on earth there isn't nothing at all nice,
about being burned by dry ice.

Ever have coffee with a fly? I have.

It was during the Muslim Holy Month of Ramadan 2006, I was a prisoner in California State Prison Delano. It was one of the last ten nights and I was up awaiting the acclaimed "Night of Power". A night wherein Angel Gabriel and other Angels come down bestowing God's blessings on those awake.

Tablet in front of me on my Upper bunk, pencil in hand, bed chest high, with a small cup of coffee at my right. As I stood pondering life's mystery, suddenly a fly lighted on the far right side of the cup. I watched as it made its way counterclockwise half way round to the front of the cup. Then I watched as it consumed a droplet of coffee. The droplet disappeared from the cups edge, appearing in the fly's abdomen. I was in awe of such an event. Then it took off. Without regard I partook of a sip of coffee, placing the cup back in his place.

Again the fly returned, lighting on the same spot, walking in the same direction to the front of the cup, and again drinking another droplet of coffee. Still overwhelmingly intrigued, I again observed this marvel. Then again the fly took flight. Without regard I again sipped from the cup. After setting it down I noticed that there were no drops on its rim. So I dipped my index finger in the brew and placed a droplet on cups edge. Again the fly return to the same landing spot, and again proceeded counterclockwise to the front of the cup, and consumed one last drop then left.
Inspired I started writing, thus was born......

The Fly

There's a creature that's not very shy,
Commonly known as the fly.

Wherever food, water material, waste matter, or men lie,
Everyone is quick to see the fly.

Busier than the bee,
Ever so quick to light is he.

Even on things that have smells man can't stand,
The fly is ever so quick to land.

Of fluids of filth and stink,
The fly is ever so quick to drink.

Never does he complain to his Lord,
Nor does he leave anything unexplored.

Not ever ungrateful is this beast,
Although of creatures he's the least.

Totally repulsed and scoffed by man,
The fly is fed by God's hand.

Before you strike him stop and think,
For he merely in search of food and drink.

Of his work and duty he never jerks or gets bored,
For he's always grateful to his Lord.

So now will hope you'll consider,
How humbly he lives off your litter.

Or when you're obnoxious and proud,
Look at the fly's way, which screen humble aloud.

And when you are an emotional ungrateful wreck,
Recall the way of the fly who's humbly grateful as heck.

While time does yet remain,
The attitude of the fly you need attain.

Whether he eats before you or behind,
He the fly does not mind.

And with others fighting is not his flare,
For he's always willing to share.

Ever so beautiful is the fly,
For we just told you why.

Through garbage and decay the fly does breed,
Successfully perpetuating his seed.

Because of his humility indeed,
The fly is destined to succeed.

Seemingly one of God's simplest of creatures,
To man is the fly one of his greatest teachers.

So when from gratitude you find yourself torn,
Think of that which the fly is born.

Through the fly you we warn,
Although Him you detest-fully scorn.

Hopefully you will heed the creature that's not very shy,
Commonly known as the fly.

He asks no questions nor tells any a lie,
For he is the humble little fly.

It matters not what you think or feel,
Because the way of the fly is a big deal.

Now is time this lesson to close,
For to you a revelation of wisdom did we expose.

So for now do we say goodbye,
To the humble teacher…The Fly.

The Fair Weather Friend

Living in a world of make-believe and pretend,
So there goes the fair weather friend.

With you he's constantly cool,
Cause he takes you for a fool.

When it comes to deceit he's a quick learner,
And he keeps his marks on a back burner.

Yes he's fast to ask you for a favor,
For the devils his lord and savior.

Yet his target rarely does he miss,
And on your ass he'll place a kiss.

When it comes to wit he is sharp,
And he'll play you like a harp.

He's your buddy while things are good,
Yet his heart is made of wood.

Living in a world of make-believe and pretend,
So there goes the Fair Weather Friend.

The Epiphany of the Prophet
Of Nur: Divine Light
(27 Ramadan 2006)
Written after 666 The Mark of the Beast-Unleashed

From the Giver of Grace,
The Creator of hell's space.

Has come to live,
To whom mercy does God give.

For in order to have clarity of sight,
One needs to have a degree of Light.

For years you've been told many a story of old,
Yet for the fire ye remain bold.

Continuously believing you're right,
Against God you fight.

Ye have failed to remember,
That to the Lord you will render,
Your spirit through death's surrender.

Staying as busy as a bee,
Misusing thy will, which is free.
You will surely soon see the inescapable reality.

The Lord took a man who was of waste full and unsure,
Then turn him into manure,
For the promise of God is sure.

From amidst the darkness of night,
God has brought forth light,
Guidance to what's right.

For to Our servant we sent a sign.

Behold while Muneer did pray,
We had caused a dust ball to circle the way
He moved his index finger while he did say – Shahadah.

Then during the month of burning, Ramadan,
Up on the third utterance of thanks from Muneer,
Did We make thunder appear.

"I want a thank You for letting me be myself again",
Is what preceded the thunders end.

From amongst yourselves God has raised a warner,
Of him many are a mocker and scorner.

Although the sins of his past were great,
He repented before it was too late,
So many of you toward him, you vent hate.

It's now time for us to state,
That in fact it's Us you resentfully hate
For Our light is painfully great.

Behold the hour,
Of which God again demonstrates His power!

Enabling a man to live,
As one whom God did forgive.

For many of you it's too late,
For you've overindulged and drowned in hate.

Then you exclaim:
By whose power has risen this man to fame
after all of his past shame?

Dare thee challenge the power,
The power of God hand rising,
Is this to you surprising?

Moses was a man,
Who killed another by blow of the hand,
And had fled the land.

He knew not he was on his way,
to be a Prophet of God one day.

Out of the muck and mire of a filth and stink,
Has God raised anew a Prophet causing man to rethink.

In order to guide you aright,
God sends forth Nur, His Light.

For your will with God's to be one,
He anew has raised the Sun.

Bearing several messages of truth,
for the guidance of the uncouth,
Whose actions We reproof.

Some say Muneer is out of his head,
and deserves to be dead.

So We say unto you,
If this were true,
It will also apply to you.

Ye have yet to see,
The marvel of Our forgiveness and mercy.

Just look at him,
Whose life and past was grim,
Living once upon Hell's rim.

Yet with a word we said,
We have raised him from the dead,
Promising him Heaven for a bed.

In many are hearts so hard and cold,
That God they dare to ridicule and scold.

Doubting the infinite Power of God,
On His warnings they trample and trod.

Living under Satan's seductive spell,
bound are they for Hell,
The truth we tell.

Of Muneer's Prophet Hood and God ye demand proof,
By some Biblical Ben Hur movie spoof.

Behold the miracle is not hiding,
Just read his writing,
For in him We're residing.

Behaving in a way so insolent and bold,
thinking the fire will one day go cold,
To you the lie has Satan told.

To those who have faith now,
at life they dare not cow,
For to Allah they say "Wow"!

Any and all will believe the truth,
when with Judgment Day come the irresistible proof.

Many are already free,
for their Faith is their key.

So ye ask, who is this one in thy sight?
Behold it is Muneer (Nur), the Prophet of Light.

For he's the man whom We've raised to be the reviver,
Of every soul destined to be a survivor.

For they will pass over Hell,
with a lightning speed this We foretell.

The message, which to you Muneer has told,
is not one new but of old,
Yet for the fire you're so bold.

If Heaven you want to be a receiver,
now's the time to be a believer,

In the Prophecy of the Mahdi.
To some the idea was a slam,
The talk of the last Imam.

For years he was hidden,
on his back Satan's ridden.

This was true,
to keep him from view.

Into Our mercy he-did We receive,
His burden of Satan did We relieve,
And with him you We retrieve.
So now are you of those who believe?
Behold We have sent you the Prophet of Nur i.e. Divine Light,
That you may be guided aright!

And again I write

Not knowing where to land,
Or whence I took flight.
I continue to stand,
And again I write.

As pristine as a summer's dove,
The branch on which it light.
I journey toward transcendent love,
And again I write.

Portrait of destiny's eve,
Itch of mosquitos' bite.
Moreover do I believe,
And again I write.

Amassing tremendous strength,
Caught within uneasy plight.
Praying at huge length,
And again I write.

Still I seek to know,
From early day to night.

Expanse of heart I grow,
And again I write.

The Adult Child

And now will mention something gone wild,
The dilemmas state of the adult child.

An entity claiming to be adult because of physical years,
A condition so sickening it moves many to tears.

Living on a reputation of so called prideful achievements,
Suffering from intense spiritual bereavements.

Appearing to the naked eye to be alive,
on the rotten inside maggots thrive.

The problem and answer you claim to know that two,
Yet bringing them together and living in solution you can't do.

Out of touch with how to freely give,
many stumble through life knowing not how to live.

The most ungrateful creature man tends to be,
when a legend in his own mind is he.

Having devolved into a legendary beast,
His soul is damned to say the least.

Today's learning

Feeling as caught up as a hype,
My drugs in coffee instead of a pipe.

I counted my chickens before they hatched,
In controversies turmoil was i catched.

What unfolded was a real life drama,
Boy I needed advice from Mama.

Easy felt and plainly seen,
Are the effects of caffeine.

When the warning came I heated it not,
As a result I put self on the spot.

To this Behavior I'll put an end,
For to God I want to be a friend.

Yes today I ran on self will,
So I wound up feeling ill.

Even though my joy was impaired,
My wrongs were easily repaired

The Quest

There is something which above man does tower,
It's simply referred to as "The quest for power".

Every hour of every day somewhere in the world,
Man's quest for four powers energetically hurled.

Seemingly his social and security needs are out of whack,
Humility and loves compassion is what he does lack.

Wanting to be the baddest, the best or first in his class,
He's mastered the art of being as stubborn as an ass.

To the words of the wise he won't listen,
Til unrelenting pain in tears over his body listen.

Try to see to be what he ain't,
Becoming God is something he cain't .

Every hour of every day somewhere in the world,
Man's quest for Powers energetically hurled.

There is something which above man does Tower,
It's simply referred to as the quest for power.

The lost and turned out

To many one thing is very strange,
That's the concept of change.

Change for the better, the right,
Something that they always fight.

Claim to have head so full of knowledge,
Though they've never spent a day in college.

Thank you they have all the answers,
Really being the devil's dancers.

Intruding on others conversations being rude,
Call themselves' real gangster' dude.

What has happened to these Generations,
Is no more than the devil's preparations.

So stuck are they on the losing team,
A true Freedom they don't even dream.

The one thing that's true Beyond a doubt,
These people are lost and turned out.

Listen

Don't take it personal you're not that important,
Please be hateful of this portent.

Not everybody lashes out at thee,
They're merely slaves trying to be free.

Forgive yourself and forgive them too,
Let God's mercy shine upon you.

Love one another each and every day,
Be not like those who don't pray.

Fastings good for the body, mind, and soul,
Heavy is the price the evil extol.

Forget not with the Lord commands,
Refuse to heed Satan's demands.

Strive for good forever and ever more,
Know faith as never before.

The Weed

Behold here's a message from hell,
Because of God's mercy to you it we'll tell.

But before we proceed,
We know it's agreed that you like to smoke weed.

Even though at times you cough and choke,
Weed your ever so quick to smoke.

We are going to keep it real,
You smoke because you like the way it makes you feel,
And you think it's no big deal.

The reason your lips with a blunt or joint connect,
Is because you like the end result the effect.

Every time you inhale a puff of smoke,
Your spirit does nothing but cough and choke.

So now we shall describe the pain,
Which causes one to intoxicate the brain.

To put it in a way that is mild,
It's the pain of being a child.

Dues to a lack of spiritual proficiency,
You've developed a spiritual deficiency.

Meaning that you've yet to mature,
Which is to gain the power spiritually to endure.

To absorb the highs, middles, and lows encountered throughout life,
So to marijuana you're a husband or wife.

Calling out from the pit of hell,
To you the truth we tell.

Really into yourself deeply indeed,
Thinking only of yourself you smoke weed.

In many areas you are smart yet to spiritually
your damn sure stupid,
So into yourself as though shot by cupid.

America, land of the free and x home of the braves,
The Indians lost their land because to weed some were slaves.

Whether its crystal meth, crack cocaine, heroin, alcohol, or weed,
A drug is a drug is a narcotic indeed.

No matter if it's used by needle, pipe, joint, or cup,
They all affect you from the neck up.

Of course it makes you feel good,
For being a narcotic it should.

A drug that dulls the senses,
Relieves pain and induces profound sleep of the spirit, body or mind,
Is no more than of the narcotic kind.

Again no matter if it's crystal, crack, heroin, alcohol, or weed;
They're all of the narcotic breed.

They all cause the user to feel good,
Due to the nature of drugs they should.

Once getting high you develop a dependency,
No longer do you have clemency.

Meaning that no matter where on earth you may be,
You are no longer of the free.

As a result of smoking bud you've put your foot through the door,
Now other drugs you're subject to explore.

Some get "cottonmouth" indeed,
After simply smoking some weed.

Thirsty now they begin to think,
And pick up a beer or cooler to drink.

Now the amount of drugs they use is two,
Don't go yet hear us through.

If you've already started getting "high" it's too late for prevention,
So how to heal your soul and recover a life we'll mention.

First we have some facts to state,
For to your condition we do relate.

Fact one is: In life pain isn't an option,
But suffering is.

Fact two is: If in life you learn not how to endure pain,
Then a child forever you'll remain.

Fact three is: That spiritual growth comes after pain,
If heaven you'd like to attain.

We must say that man was created to surrender,
To God and or mammon service he'll render.

Duty you owe to the Creator,
Yet you serve that which came later.

Needing to Gain One's Divinity,
Is the first you serve of a trinity.

Getting One's Desires is the second of the three,
Of which you need to get free.

And the last of the three for those who've lost hope,
Is those who've Gotten On Dope.

The acronyms of the three g.o.d.'s whom you seek to please,
Are merely symptoms of your spirits disease.

Stumbling your way through life like your blind,
You need to follow your first mind.

Focusing on the messenger rather than the message,
Denying thyself the mercy of God's Bless-age.

Having caused and suffered much pain,
Choosing weed over God is insane.

If an inversion of your priorities does not occur,
The torment of hell fire you will incur.

Using your hands to contribute to your destruction,
Having fallen prey to Satan's seduction.

The drinking of smoke into your hide,
Is no less than slow suicide.

Doing that which is dangerous to your life and your health,
Practicing suicidal behavior by stealth.

Surely man is unable to do his best,
While he is yet under the influence of "stress".

In order to be of those who in life succeed,
You'll need to surrender the weed.

So this to you with love we tell,
So you can break the Devil's spell.

Now if to these words of truth you don't listen
Then your soul you'll be dissen.

Ever think about or ask why you were born?
Or the fact that one day you'll answer one day to death's horn?

The period of time called life will quickly pass,
Keep getting high you'll lose your ass.

Again if you desire to truly succeed,
Surrender to God not the weed!

Fitting in

Desiring to be a part of or to fit in,
I'll talk Vanities and embrace sin.

Then in an effort to be cool,
I'll sit up and act a fool.

When It's they I try to please,
I merely increase my heart disease.

As I struggle to escape hell's fire,
I'm engaged in war with desire.

Within there are two powers that be,
Both want dominion over me.

As they come and as they go,
I play my part in life's show.

Desiring to be a part of or to fit in,
I'll talk Vanities and embrace sin.

Before my demise meaning my end,
To my Creator I hope to be a friend.

Desiring to be a part of or to fit in,
I'll talk Vanities and embrace sin.

At long last

Worry worry fear and doubt,
That's the business my head is about.

Pace tap my fingers or pick my toes,
When it comes to desire open is my nose.

Not knowing whether I said or did the right thing,
Knowing that is trouble I'd bring.

Answering questions when I wanted to cowl,
Shooting my response was really foul.

About the future in my freedom do I worry,
My thoughts and emotions propound in a flurry.

Having incurred the wreckage of my past,
Hoping to be forgiven at long last

Am I crazy?

On me the devil did cast a spell,
As I descended to the bottom of Hell.

The greatest of pain, sin, and suffering I came to know,
So I could help you all grow.

The Kingdom of Heaven you can attain,
If you follow your heart instead of brain.

The Kingdom of Heaven is within;
If to God you'll be a friend.

The Kingdom of Heaven is within,
Therefore on earth does it begin!

Our Father who art in Heaven today,
God's inside you this I say.

Your body is a temple meaning church,
So come down from the Devil's perch.

No man can come to the Father but by the Sun,
Putting you in darkness Satan has done.

No slave will ever get free,
Unless you heed the guidance from me.

When you practice religions that you don't understand,
Satan has you well within his hand.

Ignorantly practicing religious jive,
Into Spiritual Darkness did you dive.

In that darkness Satan can rule,
By appearing as an Angel of Light as a tool.

So he's mislead many of you,
So God's only Sun is here too.

To rise from being spiritually dead,
Please heed all I have said.

For right now Armageddon's war has begun,
Are you ready for the return of the Sun?

Ignorance is another word for darkness – True,
So God has again sent His Light or Sun for you.

If you don't believe that it's me,
Open your heart so you can see.

The time has come to be born a new,
And of false worship to be threw.

Should you heed what I have said,
Then you're willing to rise from dead.

Some of us have been down so long,
That we think it's where we belong.

Getting up hasn't even crossed any mind,
For centuries we've been entangled in Satan's twine.

I don't want your money or your praise,
I'm here to help you have better days.

Reverend, Pastor, Deacon, Priest, Rabbi – "Do Wrong",
Want what's in your panties, boxers, and even thong.

I don't want your money or your sex,
Into Triple Darkness have you been vexed.

There is nothing you can do or say,
that would stop me from loving you anyway.

Into death's darkness did you dive,
Your Soul I've come to revive.

It doesn't matter what's on your face, body, or head,
For you've existed as the Spiritually Dead.

Should from death you don't want to be raised,
They continue to let the Devil be praised.

Money for my ministry I wouldn't accept,
Work as a carpenter is how I kept.

Reverend Do-Wrong wants your praise,

Money, and honey,
The truth I've stated isn't funny.

Be in the world not of the world did I say,
And in prayer are you to stay.

Listen all you my fellow men and friends,
Say not Amen for then prayer ends.

The two prayers in Bible that I said,
Thy will be done is how they've read.

Thy will be done is what's to be said,
For with Amen your prayer becomes dead.

Amen means: May it be so,
Heed me so you can know.

Should thoughts and fears race through your mind,
Meditate so the stillness you can find.

Be still and know "I am God" was said,
Meditate to quiet your ever-busy head.

If a mind free of fear and day meres you want,
Then be still and mount your hunt.

Hunting for the Peace we all yearn,
Is found when inwardly you turn.

Stop looking for God in the world or sky about,
For He's with in you without a doubt.

It's not for me- you to convince,
Simply Am I crazy or do I make sense?

No Matter

No matter how many push-ups to your routine do you apply,
One day you will surely die.

No matter how much you may get buff,
To a steel blade your skin isn't tough.

No matter how hard you deliver a punch,
To a lion you're nothing but lunch.

No matter how you walk or your arms swing,
You know more than human being.

No matter how super you are of a man,
Death will take you just as planned.

No matter how bad you think you are,
Destined are you to ride in a funerals first car.

No matter what if your attitude gets worse,
Soon you'll lie in the back of a hearse.

No matter what you do or say,
To God you need practice to pray.

No matter how many push-ups to your routine do you apply,
One day you will die.

No matter how much weight you can lift,
One day through your body will maggots sift.

No matter what you think that you know,
You'll never be able to block death's blow.

No matter how much pain and hurt you to others can deal,
It's also something you can feel.

No matter how many others of you may fear,
Death is going to dig out your rear.

No matter how much you may be down,
Soon you'll be dust in the ground.

No matter what you own or how much you have,
At your ways the Devil does laugh.

No matter what remember Goliaths bullying touch,
For little David of death packed much.

Fleeting Life

At times the life of this world seems cold,
Either you die young or you grow old.

When it comes to reasons voice,
To the way of life we've no choice.

Mattering not what men may invent or try,
In spite of it all we will surely die.

You can hold your breath until you're blue,
It still wouldn't change what'll happen to you.

So why chase lives pleasure until no end,
When sooner or later you'll be death's friend.

Should with fortune you have a meeting,
Beware for in fact life's fleeting.

Contact me with questions or concerns:

isa aka jesus@gmail.com

Authors Comments

Jesus worked as a carpenter, he did not take money for his ministry and he did not sleep with members of his congregation. Like Reverend Do-wrong, Minister Pimp-along and Father Sleep-Along.

Of course some of you are questioning my Sanity.

Christians and Muslims both believe in Jesus (Isa), having come before and in his return.

Minister preach it wrong, Reverend got it wrong, Pastor pimp-along and television The One eyed devil (Al-dajjal)- The Digital misrepresentation of God and I, have their congregation waiting for a white guy to come out the sky performing Hollywood special effects miracles and saying… It's me JESUS!!!!

In today's Bible Christ is said to "Come like a thief in the night".

Furthermore it says in the book of revelations "His (Jesus) hair was white as wool" meaning nappy, and his (Jesus) skin "is like brass/bronze burned in the fire". Meaning he was black, when you burn something it doesn't turn white!

I am not back empty handed I have more Good News, Injil, Gospel.

The Bible says: " If a Prophet's Prophecy does not come true do not fear (RESECT) him, if his Prophecy comes true fear (RESPECT) him.

My writings ARE their own proof.

Muslims- The Holy Quran says: Isa (Jesus) will be a sign of the coming of the hour of judgment.

Prophet Muhammad (P.B.U.H.) is quoted as saying: The Sun (Jesus) will rise in the west.

I AM NOT NOR DO I CLAIM TO BE GOD!

1. I am here to clear my name-For my teachings have been crucified!
2. To prove to the world that I am but a man.

3. To unite the one Ummah of Prophet Muhammad (P.B.U.H.)
4. To bring Peace on earth.
5. To end poverty and world hunger.
6. And to do some other things

There is no such thing in Allah's Hadith as a Sunni, Shiite or any other type of Muslim. Allah says in HIS HADITH THE HOLY QURAN: **I HAVE MADE YOU MUSLIM. (PERIOD)**

The people of the book and other believers cannot come into a divided family. There is no such thing as a type or kind of MUSLIM. Either you are a **MUSLIM** or you are a **Great hypocrite.**

The only writing guarded and protected by ALLAH and endorsed by Prophet Muhammad Is the Holy Quran.

Any other Hadith or Sunnah or Fiq writings or "Schools of thought" That contradict or conflict with the *CLEAR* parts of the Holy Quran or that causes division (Shaytan) between Muslims...**IS TO BE THROWN OUT.**

Allah's curse is upon anyone who refuses to comply. You will be burned in the lowest depths of the Hell Fire if you continue to keep the UMMAH DIVIDED. I look forward to the Believers themselves killing you for sabotaging our Muslim Family period.

O Muslims The Holy Quran is the final revelation of Allah, and Muhammad the last Prophet. The paradox is that I Isa (Jesus) came before Muhammad with the Gospel. Would I not return with more Injil/Gospel?? When Allah raises a Prophet, He raises one from amongst the people whom the Prophet is sent to and who speaks their language.

Allah also takes the lowest of the low and raises them to be the highest of the high. Case in point. In the time of Moses the lowest one could be was a Murderer. Did not Allah raise Moses to be His Prophet?

Next I'd like to settle the dispute in our family.

The Holy Quran in Arabic is Poetry, however Prophet Muhammad was not a poet because he did not write it. He was taught it and recited that which he was taught.

The End of the Christian Error

" Breaking The Cross" O ye that call yourselves my footstep

CHRISTIANS

Nowhere in your Bible did Jesus say to be a Christian.
A Christian is Christ Like, one who practices living the way Jesus did.
Was Jesus a Christian no; in your Bible Jesus was a JEW,
He did not eat pork,
He prayed on his face.
He shunned material wealth, he did not take money for his ministry nor did he sleep with members of his congregation.
He rested on the Sabbath (Saturday),
And he upheld and practiced the Ten Commandments,
He said your body is a Temple meaning Church.
Judaism has been corrupted. The Yiddish are not the original Jewish people. The Ethiopians and many other Blacks are.

5. To conquer the one-eyed devil… the television, which has and does program the mind of so many.

Not only is Jesus back,
Like the first time he's black.

The Bible says out the darkness came the light,
Therefore Adam and Eve weren't white.

Surrender to Truth don't fight,
He's here to set the record right.
The beginning of a new day starts as night.

666 The Mark Of The Beast-Unleashed!

**This was the first piece I wrote, and I was in LA County Jail at the time.
33 pages the night of June 6, 2006 or 6/6/06
Coincidence?**

Greetings from a lifetime resident of Los Angeles County
A.k.a. the County of Lost Angels.
The breeder of many damned and lost souls.

Whether I look to the right or left I see
People vie to be happy.

Yes sad but true most of wound up feeling blue,
Or in the agony of defeat cried, "I'm too through".

Amidst all the struggle, suffering, and strife,
lies the seed of life.

O how earnestly one can pray,
when the self wants what it wants anyway.

Foolish attempts to manipulate or con God,
Begging painfully wishing He'd spare the rod.

The fact is that so so many are ill,
the direct result of misuse of the will.
Living a lifestyle that won't help but kill,
Disillusioned pursuing a superficial thrill,
having no concept of what truly real.

Breeding, grooming, and consuming all that they can,
Devoid of their purpose here as man.

Recklessly careening off the road of life,
Ready to sacrifice their self with Satan's knife.

Please be patient in time you'll see,
what message 666 conveyed to me.

Stop fighting the force of which you can't yourself free,
Surrender to the one who created thee.

The beast walks the earth in the form of man,
seeking to sabotage God's unyielding plan.

Here is a message for the chosen few,
the mercy of God sent through me to you.

Till now the cud of deceit you had to chew,
The Mark of the beast is to be unleashed to you.

So in the meantime what shall ye do?
Pray for God's will be done in the life given you!

Some say these are the ramblings of a man babbling on,
that my mind is truly gone.

The beast has attacked man at his foundation,
the sole means whence comes forth a nation.

The Womb demeaned by the word **P. U. S. S. Y.**
Put **U**nder **S**atan's **S**eductive **Y**oke,
This is by no means a joke.

The mirror holds the image of the god to whom you're true;
don't go yet hear me through.

Throughout the journey called life,
you misunderstood the purpose of one called wife.

I come bearing a message from the Father you see,
a necessary passage through the womb to be free.

First let's pop **bubble number I,**
O ye slaves of the sun.

The Bible says that out of the darkness came the light,
Therefore Adam and Eve were not white.

Surrender to the truth don't fight,
we are only setting the record right.
Remember the beginning of a new day starts as night.

Humbly ask God to remove your fears,
and seek His will with your remaining years.

Remember those fairytales you thought you knew to be true,
Like Santa Claus, Snow White, and the Smurfs, which were blue
And how you knew you were right.

Turns out it was your perception, a deception, conception of an alternate reality,
Of which later you became free.

Only the seekers, the chosen will proceed, for the haughty,
Self-righteous cannot heed.

Now those who calmly remain have entered the light,
the while the others still fight.

Struggling in the pursuit of having their way,
blind to the will of God each day.

A day in the eyes of God is one thousand years.
Remember the story of Jesus's glory.

They say he died on the cross and rose on the third day.
The sun rose while it was still dark!

Since the year 2001,
the third day of God has begun,
Are you ready for the return of the Sun?

Now it's the time for the rising of the Sun of God,
The Light, the Way, and the Truth.
No this is not uncouth.

We are six years plus into the third day,
the new way.

Take a moment this truth to concede,
Ask God that you may heed.

My name is Muneer, which means enlightening,
and what we say to the Devils is frightening.

I am the bulb, the pin the filament, and this writing the Light (Nur),
Are you with us, are you alright?

Are you ready to proceed?
Iqra iqra, means read read.

Absorb the light,
that you may learn to recite.

The beginning of a new day starts off as night;
do ye have eyes yet no sight?

Oh how the Lord is merciful unto you,
the words we write are very true.
Oh how ye delight,
Believing you know that you're right.

It's time to be born anew,
and of your arrogant self be through.

"I know" are the words the prideful say,
Closing their mind to God's will today.

Pray:
Oh Lord enable me to learn to listen that I may heed and proceed,
Remove my arrogance whereby the truth I'll concede.
My Lord remove from me the painful confusion and fear,
that leads to my pitifully shedding a tear!

Claim ye to know what ye know not,
burning with a lust steeped in the hell so hot.

Stirring in your own juices you say not,
yet you bear the stench of rot.

The heat of decay is unyielding to you,
Yet to God it will give way,
Once you rightfully live and pray.

We pray if it be God's will that you'll succeed.

To the self that can't be satisfied,
the heart, which remains, ungratified.

We bring forth more truth,
yet the unbelievers plot and plan,
against the second coming of the son of man.

Oh lost soul we have heard your cry,
yet the answer to your prayer is NO! We'll tell you why.

First listen to what your works (actions) say:

I don't want to be me,
Longing for that which I see.

The head is busy thinking;
soon I'd be drinking.

With life dis-eased,
With God displeased.

He won't help me because I've been too bad,
stagnant, waiting to follow another fad.

Wanting to rule,
superficially I'm hip, slick, and cool.

More than meets the eye,
another day to live a lie,
I want Heaven but refuse to die.

I don't want to be me,
Longing to get free.

Michael J's money, Billy Dee's honey, Richard Pryor's funny-
All in one me sheer fantasy.

Trouble to my dismay,
Tyranny agonizing a hundred fold each day.

Oh how deadly a reputation can be,
Centered in the mind of the arrogant you see.

Slavery of the severest kind,
having working eyes yet are blind.

She has money he has gold,
Underneath there's a story that goes untold.

We say to you draw from the Power supreme;
to some it's only a dream.

Deep within the heart of man,
is One with the unyielding plan.

The power needed,
to accomplish life succeeded.

If only you would heed,
through surrender do you succeed.

Living in a society, which teaches to numb all pain,
Small wonder you have no spiritual gain.

In the midst of suffering we cry to God sincere and true,
Then for us is done which only He can do.

Then we go back to doing the same,
As though we never called upon His name.

Look at how short our memory tends to be,
when from the pain God sets us free.

Having sight yet no vision the heart is hardened
With darkness through and through.
The mirror holds the image of to who you're not true.

Yes your self-serving efforts to play God
Have systematically resulted in an emotional nod.

Hold it!
There is another who you serve true,
who can only be found inside of you.

She's the downfall of many nations,
the source of many confrontations.

And exists in many whether straight or queer,
and goes by the dreadful title called FEAR!

She's being born every time there's an inability
To trust and rely on God,
Where self is dependent on but fails to do the job.

From your peace fear enjoys to rob,
just study the teachings of Bill and Dr. Bob.

To those who have an ear,
Let him hear.

For now we'll present the proof,
that what we say is truth.

When fear is at the core of what one calls life,
there is misery, depression, worry, and strife.

Real peace, joy and happiness for which ye scurry in a hurry
always eludes you,
For fear intrudes you.

When fear says run-you run.
When fear says don't look-you don't look.
When fear says lie-you lie,
and fear even makes you cry.

Totally obedient to the subtle god called fear.
For when you're dominated by this invisible, intangible beast,
there can never be any real peace.

Fear takes you to all kinds of sordid places,
and is thriving among all races.

You see she is no respecter of race, color, or creed,
Cares not if you're wealthy or in need.

Fear has no compassion, no love, and is void of truth.
Obedience and reliance
Leads to fearful compliance.

Thus we'll pop bubble number II
Fear and faith do live in the same house!
When your faith is in your fear.

When your beliefs grounded in fiction and fantasy,
No wonder the truth can't you see,
No wonder you're not free.

Your appetites you may soothe, but never are they satisfied,
Look at those who have so much yet are ungratified.

They cry: "Forget what we need,
give us more never satisfying our greed".

This is what to themselves they believe;
the life of this world has them deceived.

Power and materialism and sex they seek to retrieve,
a heart filled with loving kindness they cannot conceive.

So many claim the Christ,
Yet when push comes to shove they deny him thrice.

Intoxicated by the oldest drugs are thee,
Referring to anger, pride, envy, and lust, greed, sloth and gluttony.

So why, why must this be?
Why can't there be peace and harmony?

Why have so many gone mad,
accusing one another of being "bad".

It's just so sad,
yet the Satan's are really glad.

We've given you glimpses of the beast and his markings,
but worry not before we're through,
Will make his mark clear to you.

Now we approach bubble number 3 so
Those who exist can begin to live,
By learning how to freely give.

The dead do walk,
and appear to hear and talk.

Devoid of feeling are they,
Unable to sense the Creator today.

Every thought, intention, and action,
Emanates from a self in traction,
what of them is human?   Only a fraction!

Oh ye people who couldn't stand for something,
oh how ye have succumbed to anything.

Something being the Truth i.e. God,
Anything being the ways of the demigod.

Here are two acronyms one full of hue,
The other having no regard for you.

S.E.L.F.L.E.S.S. and **S.E.L.F.I.S.H.** Are they,
And here is what their letters say:

Spirit **E**xperiencing **L**ife **F**orm **L**oving **E**very **S**ingle **S**oul.
For love has no conditions or price for admission.

Now for the second of the two,
Listen carefully will you:

Spirit **E**xperiencing **L**ife **F**orm **I**s **S**uffering **H**ell,
Both acronyms a lot entail.

Acts of good you do-very true,
In reality personal pleasure you pursue.

Using God until you're through,
Having Him do what you want Him to.

All you do is based on selfish motivation,
even your acts to save a nation,
How self can benefit is thy contemplation.

Seeking benefits from the Creator who you view as weak,
Thinking Him you can cheat for you believe He's meek.

After all didn't they say with His son they had their way?

They claim they took God and nailed Him to a tree,
Killing Him ever so simply.

No wonder you believe that God you can deceive,
such a ridiculous story is it that you believe.

Again we say rightly you need to learn to pray.
Request God's will when you pray,
Stop seeking to have things your way.

The crucifying of Christ is happening every day,
when you believe, teach, and practice what he did not say.

Awaken from the story of which ye vainglory.

The antichrist is the preacher who,
Takes from the congregation what he is not due.

When Christ ministered and fed the thousands they sought to make him king,
yet from them he did not accept a thing.

Carpentry is what he'd do,
to get his justly due.

There are now over 33,000 denominations,

Meaning variations (distortions) of the teachings and life of Christ.

Many claim him with word yet deny him with deed.
Take a moment to digest this unpalatable truth,
for we've just hit a rotten tooth.

We know you're confused and you're pained,
for years you've been sickly trained.

Many of you this writing will not believe,
While others till death will stay deceived.

666 The Mark of the Beast Unleashed
Is the title of this volume i.e. book,
But before we show you more foundations must be shook.

In the earthly pleasures of this world do you believe,
That's why so easy you've been to deceive.

Harlotry and idolatry are your main stay,
Asking God to do things your way.

Still you don't rightly pray
all you want is to recklessly play.

Suffering from a spiritual poverty so serious,
The pleasures of this life have you delirious.
The Truth from God, you're not even curious.

Study the ruins and books of history and learning throughout all the land,
Thus revealing the fiction and contradiction brought about by Satan through man.

Raised believing in monsters, fantasies, fairytales, and fear,

No wonder to Satan you've been drawn near.

The difference between belief in God,
And believing there is a God is plain to those who can see.

Oh what a painful piece of surgery this has come to be,
For those who are blind and yet wish to see.

And oh how painfully offensive this must be,
To those who have empty eye sockets but think they see.

Freedom from the harlotry of babbling on,
By now it's time we move along.

But before we begin, we must first take your wind.
To say of the writer that of your will,
and some him you desired to even kill.

He is but a mere messenger bearing a message for you to heed,
Please continue to read.

The only Bible some will read,
Are your actions not words but deeds.

Walking your talk is hard to do,
Especially when to self you're not true.

Look at how some claim to be saved
yet when death comes they whimper, cower, and cry,
Must we reveal to you why?

It's because they profess what they know not to be true,
It's their attempt to be a better than you.

Hypocrisy is their way;
here on earth they wish to stay.

Wanting to live here forever indeed,
the word of God they cannot heed.

At the thought of death they tremble with fear and great hesitation,
For through guilt Hell is sensed as their final destination!

Pray:
Our Lord please enable us that You and Your Truth be our contemplation,
Remove our ills and admit us to Your Nation.
Thy will be done. Amen

If you desire to fly like the birds and the bees,
Pay attention to words written and spoken like these.

The Mark of the beast is mathematically found,
A simple formula that's very sound.

Now will take a moment or two,
and ask this question of you.

What is the leading cause of death?
Misery, depression, violence, suffering, disease, or strife?
No-the leading cause of death is life.
How could God have sons when He hath no wife?

The ways of the idolaters have you seized,
Doing what you damn well please.

Unaware of the implications of your spirits disease,
Wanting everyone and everything just as you please.

Having played God for so long that you say, "bless you" to those that sneeze,
Truly offended by words like these.

Continuing to do as you please,
totally succumbed to the disease.

Playing God, punishing others and even yourself,
Subconscious manifestations done by stealth.
Oh how kind, gentle, and thoughtful you'll be,
As you attempt to control and manipulate me.

Then you will make demands, poke, and prod,
In your vain attempts to play God.

Intoxicated in mind and emotions though you may be,
The Way and Light of the Creator you cannot see.

Fortunately everything is as it should be,
For today is tomorrow's history.

When God is called "Father" it means Nourisher and Sustainer.
Look preacher God does not need you as His lawyer or explainer,
Nor has you on retainer.
Oh preacher how success you savor,
Like for God you're doing a favor.

The best any of us can be,
Is a true servant of God can't you agree?

To all those betrayed and misdirected, miseducated by corrupted leaders,
Among you are true servants of God, real succeeders.

To those in authority who knowingly preach and teach

Falsehoods and atrocities have the depths of the fire within reach.
The word of God they claim to teach,
the shore of hell is their beach.
Some this message cannot reach,
For the Lord they do not seek or beseech.

So so many are emotionally immature,
Caught and drug by Satan's lure.

Good looks, good lovers, and having money and stuff is their aim.
Living a lie and life with no shame,
constantly looking toward others to blame.

Unable to accept responsibility for the harms done to you,
They rationalize and justify their way through.

Victimizing the week,
seeking an emotional peak.

Flagrantly living to do each other foul,
they have no concept of God or real faith anyhow.

Utterances from their lips such hurtful sayings,
Are backed by the words "I was joking and playing".

Having lived as slaves for so long,
Most have come to believe it's where they belong.

Raising our children on a diet of fantasy, fear, and fiction,
Small wonder they come to live in contradiction.

Alice in Wonderland, Little Red Riding Hood, The Three Little Pigs,
All of which are called "STORIES",
Each having their share of glories.

Look at how the Satan's so bold;
Have you believing **"THE GREATEST STORY EVER TOLD"**.

The life of Christ is said to have ended in a **"CRUCI-FICTION"**,
The Faith of many rests on CONTRADICTION.

Just research the groups of Christians called the Corinthians and the Basilians,
Amongst whom "Christ worship" is alien.

For 2000 years plus the Devils have taught you to scream and shout,
"WE KILLED GOD WITHOUT A DOUBT".

These things to you we have told,
For you believe that all that glitters is gold.

Thus burst **bubble number III**,
A STORY is something made up, a LIE can't you see?

Viewing life as a game, to win is your only aim.
Thinking and acting without respect or shame.

All you want you so heartlessly you pursue,
Never able to fill the void with you.

Being such a miserable wretched thing,
Spiritual decay and sickness do you bring.

Mistreatment of others for power and economics,
Is worse than any villainess deed in Marvel Comics.

Ignorance is passed down from generation to generation,
And is perpetuated throughout the entire nation.

Foolishly harming anyone or thing,
Trying for self to make a name,
and hoping to acquire fame.

Three books from God were given to you,
The Psalms and Testaments both Old and New.

Then the Satan's known as man's enemy rival,
Comprised a book given to you called "Bible".
Now for the first time we revealed to thee,
It's open "SECRET MYSTERY".

Pay attention will you
For **Bi means two**, and **Ble is short for blessings**.
Thus **Bi-Ble** means "**Two Blessings**".

One of God,
The other of the Satanist Nimrod.

**The "Wheat and the Weeds" entwined together,
From it unity comes never.**

The first man who conquered other land,
Then exalted himself as God through a simple plan.

Osiris and Ra are of his names just a few,
Sending shockwaves of idolatry that have transcended time and space,
No wonder to Hell many race.

A dreaded abode and place to rest,
for those in their Sun–Days best.

Thousands of years ago did he begin,
The practice known as the ultimate sin.

The perpetration, imitation of the one and only God,
Began with the religion of Nimrod.

Then he, his son, and their power came to be,
That which is called "TRINITY".
Worship of the "SUN" you see,
Is the oldest form of idolatry.

Oh ye slaves of the sun, we offer thee,
the key to be free.

Yet since you been slaves for so long,
Some of you believe as slaves you belong.
All desire to be free is gone.

Enough has been said and done;
oh ye blind worshipers of the Sun.

Again look at the ruins throughout all the land,
And the books of history preserved by God for man.

What we reveal is no joke,
And heavy round thy neck is Satan's yoke.

After his death Nimrod's wife arrogantly cried,
To their son Horus that she be his bride.

Her name is Isis and through her arrogance she came to be,
The mother of all sexual immorality.

**Practiced in many localities,
SEXUAL PERVERSIONS ARE NOW REALITIES.**

Sex, Sex, Sex is basic Latin for 666,

Revealing another of Satan's tricks.

Truth and falsehood do not mix,
Revealing why the wise walk with sticks.

The pen is the staff of modern day,
Dispelling bubbles of deceit, which hinder men from the way.

Some say seeing is believing,
In truth seeing is deceiving.

For through the sight you form your own reality,
Regardless of age, sex, or nationality.

And many remain self-deceived,
In God's purpose for their being they haven't believed.

Punishing self,
doing it by stealth.
Subconscious manifestations,
Having Divine implications.

One of man's instinctual drives is sex so he can thrive.
What we say is no jive,
nor you are we apt to connive.

Into darkness did your spirit dive;
it's what we've come to revive.

Empathy, sympathy it's good your brother you understand,
It's better when you give him a hand.

You've said you wanted a Truth teacher,
Not another misdirected preacher.

Take your fingers from your ears,
Stop crying those self-pitying tears.
Ask God to remove your fears,
Start seeking Heaven with your remaining years.

Pay close attention to that which we have said,
For this powerful Light can raise the dead!

Magic, astrology, and all superstition,
Are to God's Word contradiction.

For things in this life that ye lust,
Acquiring with a currency that says:
"In God we trust".

Made in America and so it may seem,
That the color of your god is green.

Green also symbolizes envy,
Hatefully wanting more while ye have plenty.

No wonder each other love can't ye give,
In your brothers place ye long to live.
Running through life like a receiver is how ye live,
Taking from others all they'll give.

Convinced that happiness is having what you want,
Expressing ingratitude for that which ye have.
Fame, fortune, and glory,
Is the theme of your life's story.

Oh how ungrateful man can truly be,
Constantly longing for that which he sees,
Unaware of the fear within that governs he.

Materialism is what you been believing,
Indeed the pleasures of this world are deceiving.

So so many act in hopes of feeling good,
Not doing that which they should.

Born it would seem to live the lie,
For money and status to God they cry.
A monopoly and guarantee on God
And heaven they pride-fully assume,
Refusing to strap up with TNT for Him and go **boom!**

When it comes to living, fighting, and dying in the cause of God,
They do like the roaches in the middle of the night,
When is turned on the light.
Instinctively running hoping to escape God's sight,
Accustomed to darkness afraid of right.

Through our servant we reveal to you,
Something both of old and new.

On your rear you sit claiming to be in need of rest,
Knowing nothing of service living in jest.
You sit up and cry "Oh God I did try",
Thinking to Him you can lie.

America, land of the prisoners and home of the slaves.
From the city of Lost Angels We bring to thee,
An example of Our Power and Mercy.

From the lowest depths of the fire,
Dwelt one who against God didn't conspire.

Having been lost and turned out,

At the mention of God or Heaven and he'd pout.
His life was full of doubt,
And to selfishness he was devout.

After causing so many pain,
Suffering and humiliation was his gain.

A demon from the depths of hell,
On the unsuspecting he'd cast a spell.
Praying in vain did he,
For God-like he could not be.

Bearing the Mark of the beast,
He despaired of being released.

Much of the truth did he learn,
Ability to live it he did yearn.

Unable to apply that which he thought he knew,
Caused him to think that with him God was through.

Spoiled and self-willed did he stay,
Playing God each and every day.

Seeking his worldly toll,
Trying to recover his lost soul.

Instinctual perversions became his sins,
Repeating them again and again.

Then for him was done which only a mother could do,
Out of a love so pure and true.

To God was uttered her prayerful cry;
"Lord please don't let my son die in the street,

Lock him up and stand him on his feet".

And in response to what she'd pray,
A simple word did God say – okay!

So to jail is where he went,
Where to God his will was sent.
Of his sins does he repent,
On his knees much time is spent.
Daily living making amends to others,
In selfishness he no longer smothers.

Living anew thinking of others,
Not of his power but of his mothers.

Power and mercy did proceed,
To him truly from God indeed.

*

Now we intend to make known to thee,
That which before you could not see.

Some for God live to do their best,
The while others call them terrorists.

The truth is painful you see,
for from falsehood it rips you free.

The idea of being secure is what you pursue,
Regardless of what to your brother you have to do.

Which brings to mind the allegorical story or fable,
Of which Cain killed Abel.

Able lived sacrificing his best to God that he could,
Cain killed him for being good.

The wicked man just can't stand,
when the good do what God has planned.

And if they could frustrate God's plan,
They would any way they can.

Life on earth so it may seem,
is ruled by those on Satan's team.

So now more truth it's time to explore,
For we shall pop **bubble number IV**,
by breaking the Apple down to its core.

And so we will tell you something of the two,
Known as Adam and Eve to many of you.

They both were given guidance ever so pure and true,
Of what to and not to do.

Then the serpent full of deceit,
Suggested the fruit would be good to eat.

Fruit is that which bears seed,
the means by which life can reproduce or breed

Both Adam and Eve knew Good (Right) from Evil (Wrong),
Living by Good till Satan came along.

Stand before a mirror raise your arms and you'll see,

Yourself symbolizing a tree.

First Eve ate then Adam joined in,
The act called "Original Sin".

Then they "CAME" slang for "CLIMAXED"
And knew their shame,
Then covered their Fruit (sex organs) of which we won't name.

Thus we break the spell of the infamous "Apple Rumor",
Cutting it away like a cancerous tumor.

Revealed to thee nice and neat,
the story of Adam and Eve is now complete.

Take a moment or two this Truth to yourself to concede,
Ask God for strength then continue to read.

Pray: Our Lord we thank Thee for all we have in this current present moment. Amen

The 8th day

Now it's time that we expose the "God being tired jive",
By **bubble burst number V**.

In the book of many names like Tarot, Torah, Old Covenant to mention just a few,
Commonly called Old Testament to many of you.

There is a misunderstood statement in the book called Genesis of Bible,
For which the truth we have a revival.

It is written that:
"God created the heavens and earth in 6 days and on the 7th He rested".

Many have foolishly believed,
that the Creator having worked needed to be relieved.

Viewing the Creator in a humanly image,
Thinking He'd benefit from spinach.

Yet in fact the truth will now bring to thee,
So of this fallacy you can be free.

The term "rested" simply means He stopped the process of creation,
Putting all in a day of "Suspended Animation".

Establishing Himself the 7th day as Sovereign Lord,
Meaning the one who alone is King,
New truth we'll now to you bring.

For now to you we'll say,
What took place the 8th day.

On the 8th day the Creator resumed creating,
and about which this fact is beyond debating.

For life is ever renewed and freshly created,
The truth from the Lord we've just stated.

Intentions

How quick those of this world are to judge by physical appearance,
As though they've been given a heavenly clearance.

Yet they are hopelessly blind,
to what lingers in the heart or mind.

In days gone by was previously mentioned,
that the road to hell is paved with good intention.

So now will make clear to thee,
that which before you could not see.

With the eternal fate of thy soul do you carelessly play,
So now it's time to pray:

Oh Lord please help me see the truth,
for my life is in reality uncouth.

Lord I pray that Thy Will not mine is done,
whereby with You I'd be one.

Intentions without the power of readiness to act is no more than feeble wondering
Of the heart or mind,
Bringing to light the "spot" to which you been blind.

"I didn't mean to" or "I meant to" is what the well intentioned sincerely and honestly say,
Unaware of their futility, lost from the way.

Even the acts based on so-called "well-intentioned good",
Being based on self they blow up, as they should.
For these assume they know what God's will is for them and thee,
And in prayer waste time telling God what His will and should be.

These words of enlightenment are to be reviewed and diligently studied,
Until you and they are buddied.

Mental and emotional intoxication,
Have caused the fall and death of many a nation.

For those embedded in the realm of spiritual blindness,
Through the vehicle of selfishness they do kindness.

Friends they aren't to themselves or you,
Scheduled to be saved are chosen just a few.

In the worst of prisons this they've come to be,
Causing pain and damage knowing and unknowingly.

Some to whom the Spiritual Power of this writing will reach,
While others will remain a vampiric leech.

The children tend to disregard words from your lips like you're playing,
For they really hear what your actions saying.

Dangerous is the course of action some pursue,
Attempts to dominate and control the child entrusted to you.

The parent is meant to be a protecting, nurturing example teacher,
Not a dictating hypocritical controlling preacher.

A loving helpful guide,
Is the parent who aids the child on his or her spiritual ride.

In order for the children to emotionally and mentally mature,
The ultimate realities of this life they need to learn to endure.

If indeed you want thy child's footing to be sure,
Your loud actions need be a lure.

Trapped in a voraciously hungry cycle,
In need of God's help through the angel Michael.
Pray:

**Oh Lord if it be Thy will,
Separate me from my selfish ill. Amen**

For you a tear is all we will cry,
For on God you tell a lie.

Carrying on as though in a daze,
Lacking confidence seeking praise.

Wanting no more than the approval of your brother,
Yet envying the success of one another.

Like the jail house or street corner preacher,
Equal are you to Sunday's lesson teacher.

Refusing to show a sermon dead bent on talking one,
The battle against being good has evil won.

Falling at one hundred and twenty feet per second,
To the way of God have you been beckoned.

How unruly are the things you pursue,
Living against the Truth within you.

Now it's time for us to say,
How dare you think that God you can play.
If indeed the truth you wish to seek,
Then approach prayer being humbly meek.

America the 6 (Sex) Nation

In western culture adulthood is seen
As that which is entered upon age 18.

Of the stages of growth the number is three (3),
Childhood, adolescence, and adulthood to remind thee.

One cannot obtain a business name,
Or credit card on his own,
Until on his ID card the age of 18 is shown.

Of course a child or minor is seen,
As those from one second to year 17.

Add 3 to 18 is 21 so we think,
That now we're old enough to drink.

In order to unravel the mystery,
we must first divide 18 by 3.

From 0 to 6 everything is cool,
For 6 is the age for grade 1 of school

Then from 6 until you're 12,
Awareness of the world in knowledge you delve.

Then when 1 is followed by 3 you're a teen,
Who senses is and awareness is keen.

In the book of Revelation chapter 1 followed by 3 referring to the verse as seen,
Represented by the number 18.

6+6+6 = 18.

The number of the beast really does stand,
For those considered an adult American.

Revelations 13:17 points out "you can't buy or sell" without this mark that is the beast name,
Or the number 18 which means the same.

13:16 tells that every merchant or cardholder has the right in his forehead or hand,
To buy or sell throughout the land.

So now you have just seen,
the relationship between 666,

And the acquiring of money green,
and a number of the beast being 18.

www.ingramcontent.com/pod-product-compliance
Lightning Source LLC
Chambersburg PA
CBHW082249220526
45469CB00009B/2936